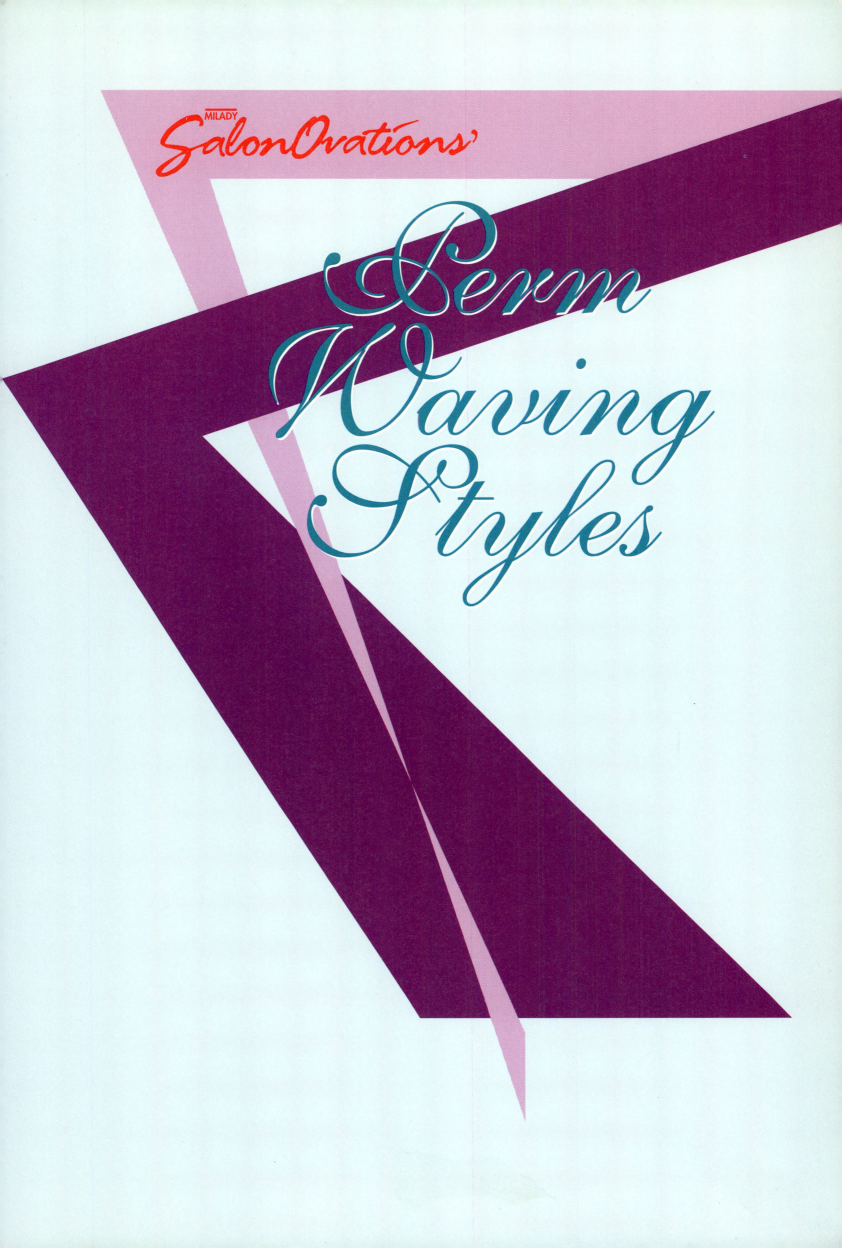

MILADY
SalonOvations'

*Perm
Waving
Styles*

SalonOvations'

Perm Waving Styles

by
Candi Ekstrom
and
Louise Cotter

Milady Publishing
(a division of Delmar Publishers)
3 Columbia Circle, Box 12519
Albany, New York 12212-2519

NOTICE TO THE READER

Cover Design: D. Dupras

Milady Staff
Publisher: Catherine Frangie
Acquisitions Editor: Marlene McHugh Pratt
Project Editor: Annette Downs Danaher
Production Manager: Brian Yacur

COPYRIGHT © 1996
Milady Publishing
(a division of Delmar Publishers)
an International Thomson Publishing company I(T)P®

Printed in the United States of America
Printed and distributed simultaneously in Canada

For more information, contact:
SalonOvations
Milady Publishing
3 Columbia Circle , Box 12519
Albany, New York   12212-2519

1 2 3 4 5 6 7 8 9 10 XXX 01 00 99 98 97 96

Library of Congress Cataloging-in-Publication Data

Ekstrom, Candi.
    SalonOvations' perm waving styles/ by Candi Ekstrom and Louise Cotter
        p.   cm.
    ISBN: 1-56253-312-6
     1. Permanent waving.   I. SalonOvations (Firm) II. Title
TT972.E39 1996   95-21219
646.7'242–dc20   CIP

Contents

2

5

6

8

9

15

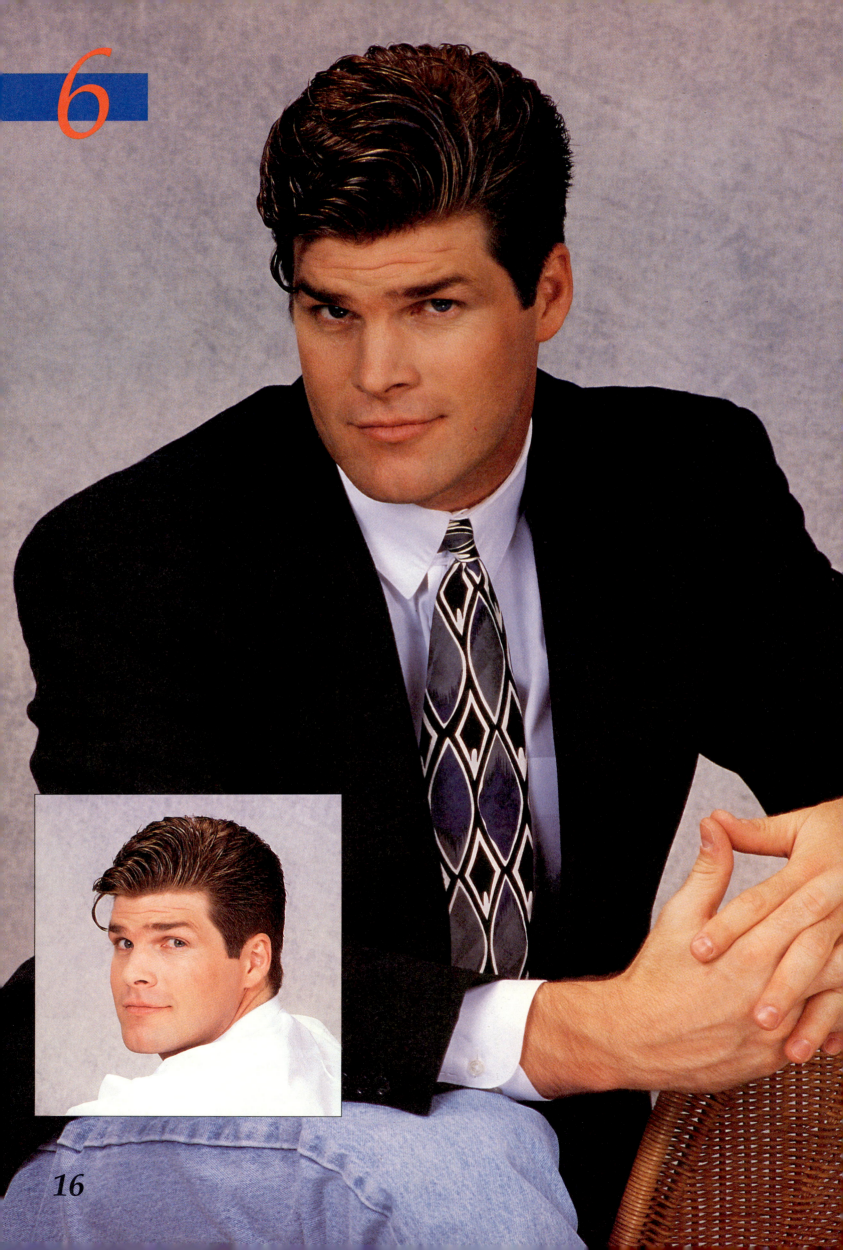

6

16

18

23

33

35

41

44

51